Starting a Wildlife Pond

by
Peter Sibley

**Illustrations by
Tessa Lovatt-Smith**

Contents

School Garden Company

1. | Why construct a pond?

There are many reasons for constructing a pond — one is that over the last 100 years over half of Britain's ponds have been drained, filled in or ruined by pollution. London has lost 99% of its ponds in this period. The result has been a tremendous loss of wildlife habitat; plants and animals once common are now rare. The only way to replace these lost ponds is by creating new ones. But ponds also have aesthetic and amenity value. People are attracted to rivers, lakes and ponds; a pond is a focal point in a garden. Many school grounds are rather featureless; a pond will add visual interest, colour and variety. Most villages had their Pond along with the Green, the Church and the Pub — putting in a wildlife pond has to be a marvellous way to get the village community together.

Part of the appeal of ponds lies in the question, what lives in there? A crystal clear pond holds no mystery. A pond is a small, self-contained world, totally different from the world we inhabit, and because of this, exotic and strange, especially to children. A pond constantly changes in response to the seasons, weather, the growth of plants and the activity of animals. In this, it demonstrates the cyclic rhythms of the natural world both daily and seasonally and also the longer sequence of ecological succession.

All of these aspects of a pond can be used to help children understand more about the world they live in, developing their power of observation and reasoning and acting as a source of inspiration for creative activities.

Lastly, the creation of a pond involves measuring, mapping, calculating, planning, research, costing, discussion of alternatives, usually some fund-raising, planting and a lot of co-operative hard, physical work! It is the kind of practical project which can involve all sorts of people. School ponds, for example, succeed best when created jointly by pupils, parents and teachers, so that a collective sense of ownership results. A successful pond is something that creates a real sense of achievement, a group effort with positive, lasting results and which all members of the family, school or community group can contribute towards.

Having said all this, be warned, there are pitfalls! The purpose of this book is to help you avoid them and create an attractive, safe pond, full of life and interest. Most of what follows applies to any type of pond, including the "ornamental" garden pond with its fountain and gleaming goldfish, but from a conservation viewpoint, wildlife ponds are what is really needed. These allow many plant and animal species threatened by the bulldozer and the crop sprayer to find new habitats — in your own bit of land to be shared again with nature.

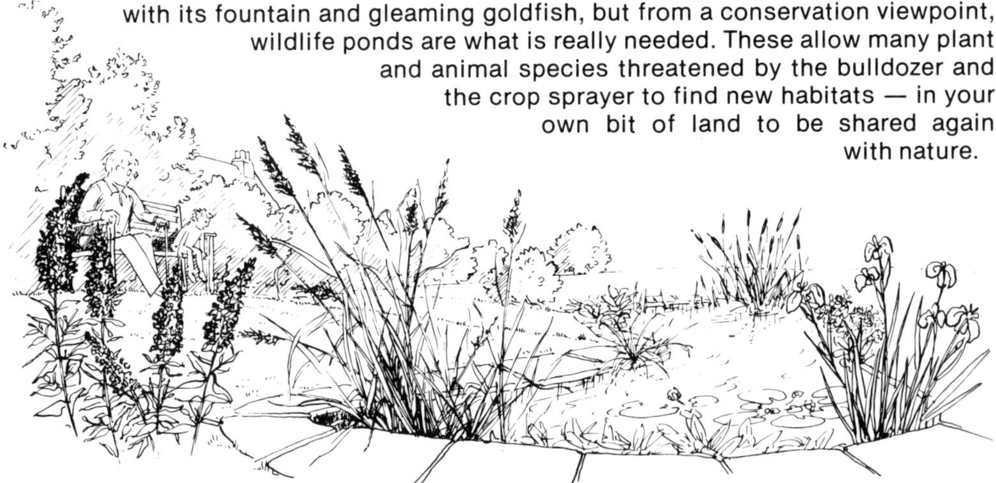

2. Planning your pond

You have decided to go ahead and create a pond? Good for you, but before you start digging there are a few things to do.

1. Consultation

It is important to consult everyone who might be involved. For a garden pond, talk the whole idea over with the family, and perhaps even the neighbours. In a school pond project check with the LEA and owners of the grounds: the governors, headteacher, other teachers and perhaps most important, the caretaker. It is also a good idea to consult the parents and any groups who use the school (in the evening for instance). Asking people usually forestalls trouble and often brings offers of help. On areas of publicly owned ground, consult the appropriate council officers and departments. You may discover an existing but 'derelict' pond site in your neighbourhood, and change your project from a new pond to a renovation! (Incidentally, ponds *don't* require planning permission, but neighbours can object to the environmental health department if they cause a nuisance).

Plan One

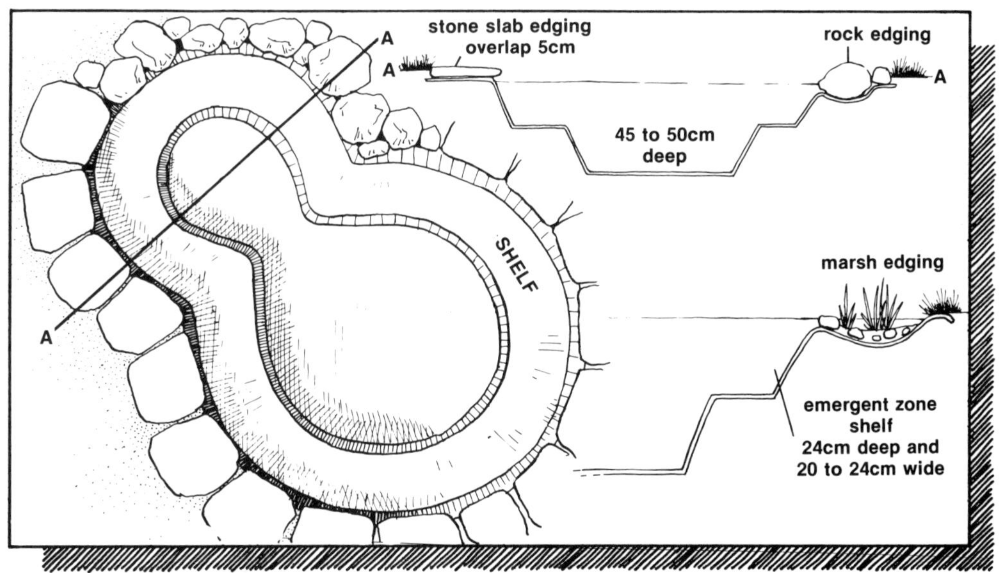

2. Planning and research

Before you start, pick your site (see the next chapter for help in this); decide on the shape, depth and profile of your pond (see next chapter again); and do a little careful test digging to find out what the ground is like.

Next, try to find out if your chosen area has any pipes, cables, sewers, drains, cesspits or old building foundations under it. (You never know what you will find; maps and plans are often inaccurate, but it is best to avoid unpleasant surprises — like power cables — if at all possible). The services companies are normally helpful in checking their plans of underground pipes, etc.

After that, try to calculate how much earth will need to be removed and approximately how long it may take; also decide what you'll do with it. Bear in mind that dug-out soil takes up more space than it previously occupied, because it is less compacted. A good idea is to build a mound or bank behind your pond; decide **where** first, to avoid shifting earth twice. If your calculations show that your mound is liable to overtop Ben Nevis, it may be advisable to make more modest plans (alternatively, call your pond a reservoir and launch your own water company).

Other factors to consider are access to the pond, an easily observed site (for safety and to avoid misuse) and shelter.

3. Costing

This is when you must try to get a rough idea of costs. Do not go to a landscaping company or professional gardening firm unless you feel very rich. (A communally built pond is usually better looked after anyway). Instead, cost your raw materials, cement, sand, flagstones, bricks, plastic pond liner, glassfibre pond, puddling clay or whatever you decide to use and the tools you'll need. Cost the alternatives too, which will either confirm or change your plans. A good method of costing is to calculate rough quantities and then phone all the suppliers in the area. (Make sure that you only ask for a quotation, do not use the term 'order' or a lorry load of aggregate may get dumped on your drive.) You will probably find that prices vary considerably. Ask about discounts. If the suppliers accept credit cards, they have to pay commission, so they'll probably give you a discount for cash.

<u>Plan Two</u> — rectangular using paving slabs

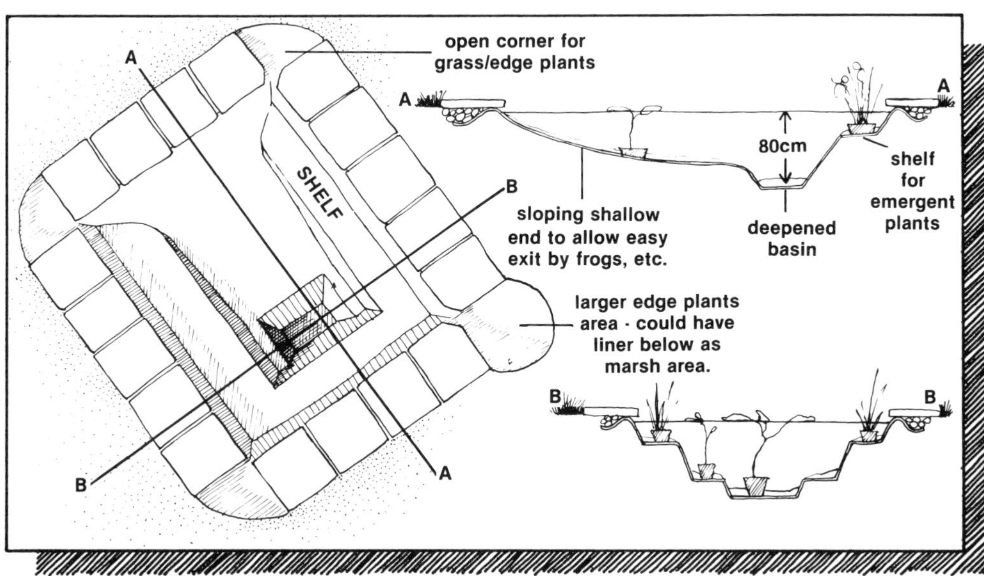

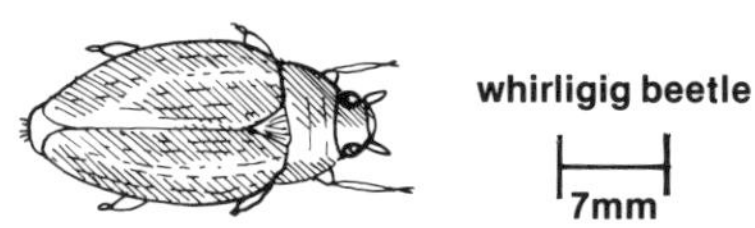

4. Type of pond

Ponds can be constructed in several ways and of many different materials; each has its advantages, you must decide which is most suitable.

Ponds can be constructed virtually anywhere — they can be built above ground, even on flat roofs. A raised pond is a particularly good idea if you are concerned about wheelchair access, the safety of very small children or the elderly and infirm. It can also be a way to build a pond on a hard surface area (rock, concrete, asphalt, tile or similar).

Another way to construct a pond is by damming a stream. If you do this, take professional advice and install a proper spillway to cope with rainstorms. This kind of pond will affect the local drainage and might create an extensive marshy area, excellent for wildlife but a problem if it affects neighbouring property.

Most ponds are, however, dug ponds lined with one of several materials. An unlined dug pond is not usually a good idea because the water level will fluctuate according to local weather conditions; it cannot be topped up artificially in dry conditions because the water will seep away until its level reaches that of the local water table.

Assuming then, that your pond is going to be a lined pond either above or below ground level, what are your options?

To take them in alphabetical order:-

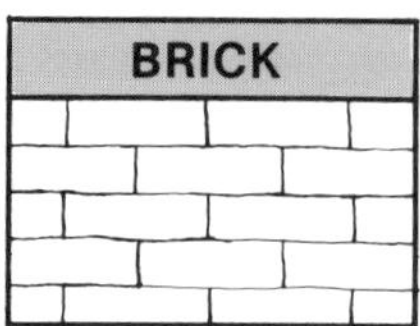

Brick

Brick is not a very practical material for constructing ponds because it is porous. It can make an excellent hard edge for a pond and weathers well. It is a good choice for the walls of a raised pond but it is better to use some other material to retain the water. Other problems are difficulties in building 'natural' curves and slopes. Wet brick tends to become slimy, which can be dangerous. Waterproofing brick is difficult, and some compounds sold for this purpose are toxic. Mortar can be toxic when fresh, also. Brick is probably therefore better avoided as a pond construction material.

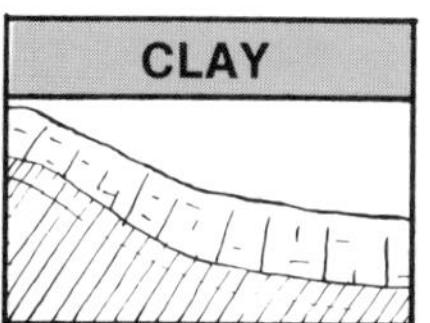

Clay

Clay is the traditional material for constructing ponds. It was used by the 18th & 19th century navigators or 'navvies' to line the canals they built and it still retains the water to the present day. Most of the old ponds in Britain were man-made using clay, whether in fields, gardens or village greens.

It is the most natural lining material available, provides an excellent substrate for waterplants, is entirely non-toxic and helps to buffer acidic or alkaline water. Those comprise the benefits.

As for the drawbacks: in order to make clay linings impermeable they must be 'puddled'. This means rammed, trampled, or trodden down until the lumps of clay coalesce to form a seamless layer. This takes a lot of hard work and can only be done when the clay is wet, which makes it very messy.

The old time canal builders used to flatten the wet clay by thumping it with the backs of shovels and then driving herds of sheep and cattle along the bottom of the canal to tread it down. (You could try holding a kid's welly boot disco in your new pond to get the same effect, but do remember how slippery wet clay is).

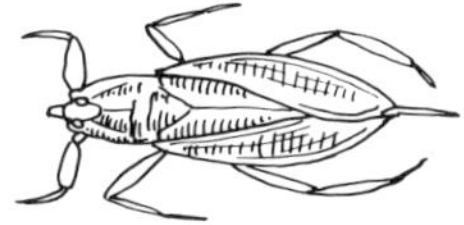

To get the best result, try to shape the clay to blocks that fit together closely and then wet them before 'puddling'. It should be pretty obvious that you need a lot of hard working volunteers for this process. You also need a very large supply of suitable clay — which is extremely heavy. If a road is being constructed in the vicinity through a clay soil the contractor may be willing to deliver a lorry load free. Otherwise the cost of transport will be high. Bear in mind that the clay must be 5 to 10cm thick to be really waterproof. If your pond dries out and the clay cracks badly you will have to repeat the puddling process.

If you do use clay, make sure that all slopes are shallow; climbing a wet clay bank is very difficult and could be fatal for a young child, an elderly, injured or drunken person. If you still decide to use puddled clay, I advise you to contact BTCV (see Appendix B) for specialist help as they appear to be the only national organisation with recent experience of using this method.

Concrete

Concrete is commonly used to construct ponds. It is very versatile as it can be formed to almost any shape, can be textured, and is also entirely non-porous. It does however, have a few drawbacks. These are: it must be about 8 to 10cm thick for structural strength; for best results the whole pond should be poured in one operation; shaping curves and slopes is not easy and *raw* or new concrete contains toxic substances that must be rinsed out by changing the water in the pond once or twice. Vertical pond walls can be cracked by ice expansion in particularly hard winters and newly poured concrete can crumble if it freezes before it is properly set. Having said this, many very successful ponds have been constructed of concrete and it has the advantage that it takes an extremely determined vandal to break it. The most usual source of any problem stems from not ensuring that the underlying soil is fully compacted; if it is not, the weight of the filled pond causes the concrete to settle unevenly and as a result, it cracks. Cracked ponds can be repaired but seldom completely successfully. Perhaps the best thing to do with a cracked concrete pond is to fill it with soil and create a bog garden, stocked with marsh plants.

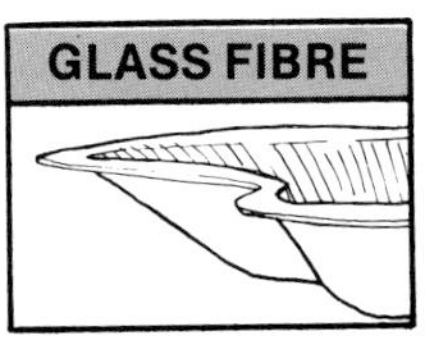

Glass fibre or GRP ponds

These are the commonest types of *ready-made* ponds, pre-formed structures that merely need a hole dug, or a raised structure built to fit them. In spite of their thin walls and light weight they are strong and long lasting, but have many drawbacks. They are limited in size and although they come in many shapes, never seem to be quite what you had in mind! They look artificial and are often pastel blue or other unnatural colours. The profile tends to be too steep and the interior surface is dangerously slippery. If the hole dug is not exactly the right shape they can warp and crack when filled and they are not damage proof. Glass fibre can however, be repaired quite easily. Depth is limited and they provide poor 'footholds' for plants. Overall they are of limited use for conservation purposes — but any pond is better than none and they do have the virtue of being quickly established. Frogs and toads don't seem to mind the artificiality and often breed in these ponds, though the steep sides can be a problem.

gnat pupa

5mm

Plastic and butyl rubber liners

This is currently the most popular method of pond construction because of its ease, cost and flexibility. A variety of different pond liners are on the market, of different strengths, lifespans and costs. Basically though, you get what you pay for. A cheap plastic liner will not last long (perhaps a few years), thicker double-sided plastic liners are more expensive but will give 10 years (or more) service, and the strongest, thickest butyl liners have an almost indefinite life. They can be made to fit almost any hole whatever the shape, are large enough to fill nearly any pond you can dig and can be repaired if punctured.

Plan three

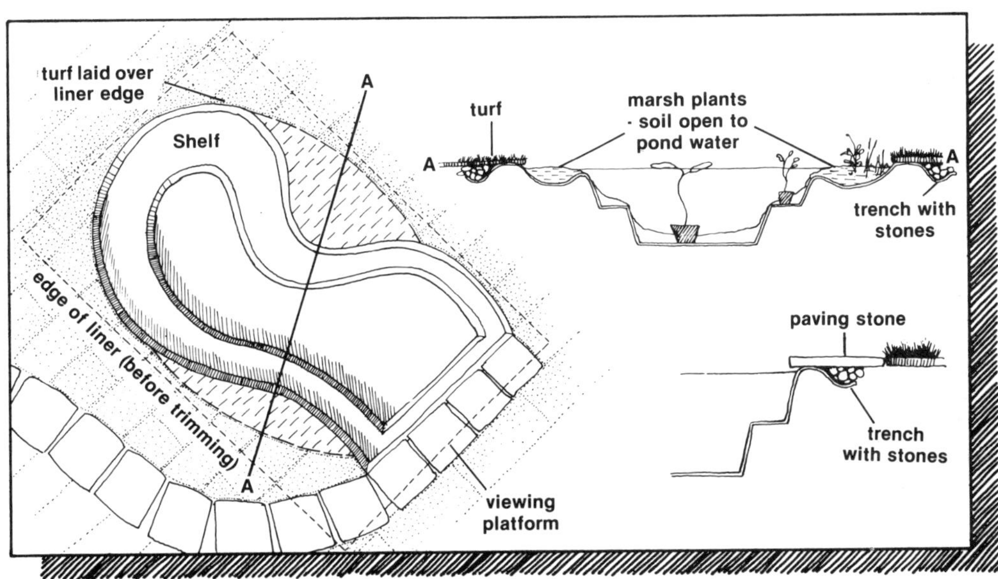

Three main types of flexible liner are available from garden centres and suppliers (see Appendix B):

Single sheet of PVC — the cheapest type available in several colours (stone, black, blue, etc.). The thicker the better, but like all PVC it is eventually weakened by sunlight (ultraviolet light). Plan your pond so that none of the PVC liner is exposed directly to light — cover edges with soil and paving stones. Black sheets are most resistant to u/v light. PVC sheets stretch to fit into corners of your pond, making installation quite simple and safe.

Double sheet of PVC — has the same eventual problems as single sheets, but the double layer sheet (often different colours on the two sides) may be more durable.

Butyl rubber sheet — most expensive but also the best sort of liner. The black butyl is thicker and heavier than PVC and although not quite so stretchy, it conforms well to pool contours. Butyl is not affected by sunlight or bacterial growth and so need not be hidden completely, though covering with soil gives a more natural appearance.

Working out the liner size — first decide how deep your pool will be. Small ponds should be around 40 to 50cm deep (in their deepest part — the pond floor should not normally be simply *flat*) and larger ponds up to 80cm deep. Only lakes need to be any deeper!

Now work out dimensions for your liner:

Length is the overall length of the pond plus *twice* the maximum depth.

Width is the overall width of the pond plus *twice* the maximum depth.

This formula will give sufficient surplus liner for the overlap at the pool edge, because of the sloping pool walls.

The biggest drawback of a pond liner is that is not vandal proof. Precautions can be taken to protect pond liners and care must be exercised in the construction of the pond to ensure a long life. Although not perfect, pond liners are probably the best option for most ponds, though in some circumstances concrete or other materials may have advantages.

Specials
It is worth mentioning here other 'ready-made' ponds, e.g. old baths, sinks, plastic or galvanised iron water tanks, old barrels, tubs, troughs, etc. All of these can be quite successful, especially if camouflaged inventively. Try a mix of 50% peat and 50% cement to disguise sinks, etc. Please bear in mind that even mini-ponds like these can be dangerous to animals, babies and toddlers, especially slippery, sheer sided tanks. Incidentally, neither lead nor copper tanks are a good idea as these materials are toxic though such vessels often develop a protective layer of scale or oxide on their surface which makes them relatively safe. The same is true of brass, bronze and pewter which are also best avoided.

If you want water in your garden but are worried about safety, why not install a fountain in a tank, tub or half barrel filled to the top with stones? The fountain will play attractively and the water run down through the stones to keep it supplied. Alternatively, a cascade could be constructed which ends in a similar stone filled pond. (Ask a qualified electrician to help with the wiring up of the pump.)

Sometimes materials are available locally, free or at normal cost. Examples might be dressed or rough stone, paving slabs, flagstones, or old kerbstones (try your local council highways dept. for these), floortiles or slate, unwanted cast concrete shapes, or other such solid material. It makes sense to use such materials and incorporate them into pond construction. Stone and concrete is cheaper than concrete alone if your stone is free, and looks better. Make sure that the stone is non-porous though! If you are offered some material and can't think how to use it, why not organise a competition for the best, most original ideas? For example, worn flagstones would make a lovely cascade, hollow breeze blocks are no good for construction but make good plant pots — the possibilities are endless.

5. Soakaway

Lastly, whatever method of construction you decide on, remember your pond is artificial: it will have to be maintained and topped up. If it rains heavily it may overflow, so a run-off channel should be provided, with a soakaway if possible.

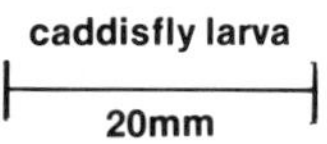

Plan four — a 2 basin pool

Constructing an overflow and soakaway.

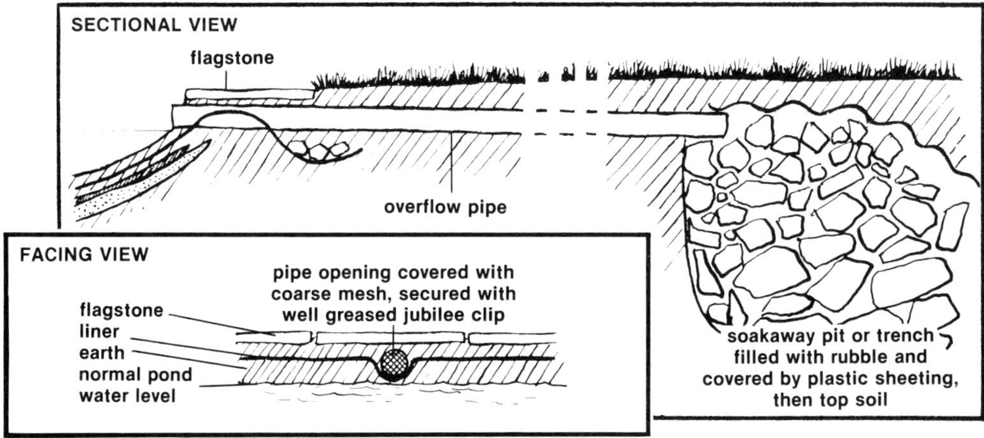

To avoid soil getting in to the soakaway from above, use punctured plastic sheeting or wire mesh before replacing the top soil.

Plan five

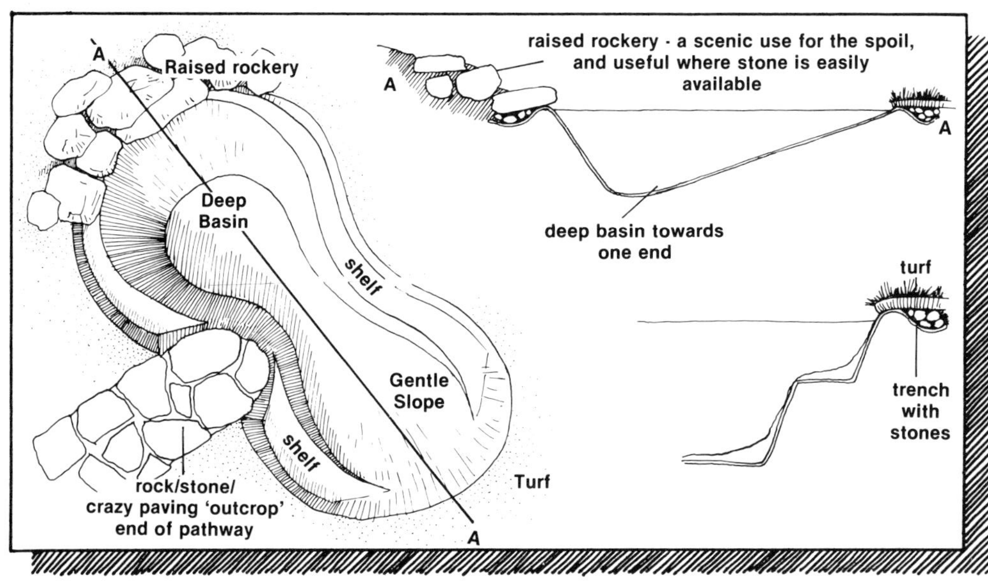

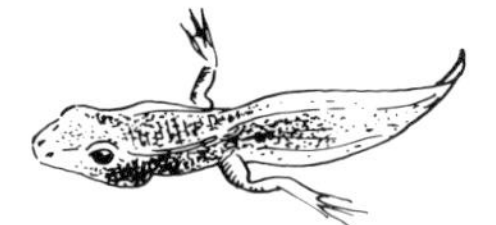

developing frog tadpole

<table><tr><td>**3.**</td><td># Building your pond</td></tr></table>

The site

Often only one site is possible for a pond, in this case you must make the best of it, but if you do have the choice of sites, consider the following factors:

Safety

The safest site is one which is not hidden away or screened from sight. The very best site for a school pond is probably in good view of the staffroom window! This ought to cut down misuse of the pond, litter dumping and the incidence of children being pushed in. For a community site, position the pond in clear view of the road, though not too close to it. Hedges, trees and other 'screens' invite problems.

Shelter

Placing a pond in the angle of some walls or sheltered by a bank helps to protect it from wind and extremes of frost. Check the prevailing wind direction, and position your spoil-heap bank in a curve to intercept it. Siting the pond under trees, however, is not a good idea since it may be too shady for good plant growth and will tend to fill with leaves in autumn. If not cleared these can kill most of the life in the pond as they rot down, de-oxygenating the water.

Shade

A pond placed in a fully shaded position, e.g. north of a high wall, will seldom have a very attractive appearance. The water will be colder than a sunny pond and the productivity lower, however it will evaporate less than an exposed, sunny pond. Small ponds in exposed, windy, sunny sites can lose a lot of water in a long, dry, hot spell. Larger ponds tend to have a lower surface/volume ratio and are less obviously affected. As a rule of thumb, position the pond so it gets at least half a day of full sun.

Slope

A pond in a natural hollow may tend to flood and overflow during wet weather. One sited in a natural run-off channel or stream bed may suffer scouring or be filled with debris during rain storms; either adversely affects the living organisms in the pond. For these reasons it is best to site the pond on a slight slope. This usually produces an attractive effect and makes it easy to arrange drainage, but may limit the shapes possible. A pond on a flat piece of ground can be any shape, but drainage is a little more difficult.

Access

Remember that your pond must be accessible, both during the construction phase and later, for use (e.g. pond dipping) and maintainance.

Think about this in particular if you are using a mechanical digger, or having ready mixed concrete or other heavy materials delivered.

The ideal situation is accessible, but not too accessible; to avoid unwanted visitors such as vandals, large water-loving dogs and rubbish dumpers.

Water
Check the nearest mains tap that can be connected up to a hose to fill and top-up your pond. Get its owner on your side, unless you have a stream available on-site.

Timing
The best time to build your pond is spring, so that it will have all the summer to get established. Ponds can be built at any time of year, as long as the weather permits, but building a pond in the winter is hard work.

Digging your pond

Having picked a site, decided on materials, checked for drains, cables, Roman remains and the like, and consulted with any appropriate interested parties, you can now organise your workforce and start a test pit. This should rapidly tell you what kind of soil you have, its depth and likely problems.

The time taken to dig the test pit should allow you to make a rough estimate of the time necessary to dig the pond. (Allow a generous margin of error, for fatigue.) Your test pit does not have to be within the area of your pond: filled with rubble it would make a good soakaway drain for an overflow. Assuming all has gone well up till now,

SECTIONAL PLAN FOR CAST CONCRETE POND

the next stage is to mark out the area of your pond. You can outline it with rope or tape until you are satisfied that you have it correctly marked out and then replace the

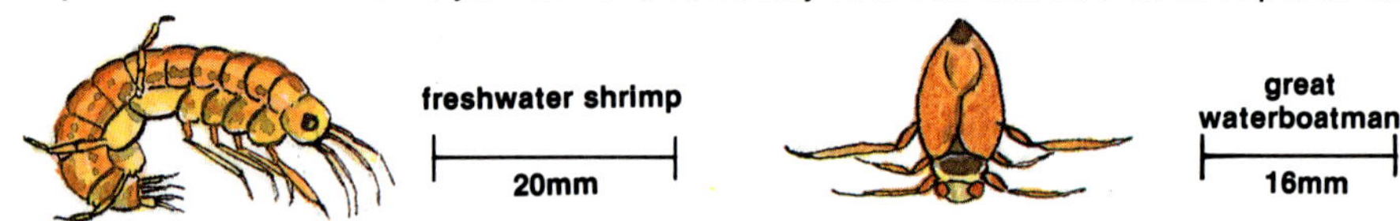

cord or tape with a white line (try powder paint or whitewash).

Now you are finally ready to start digging. Make sure that you have enough tools for everyone and that every digger knows the shape and depth profile of the pond.

If the area is covered by turf, divide it up into squares by stretching strings across it, then use a sharp space to cut the grass into equal sized turves. Use a shovel to lift the turves. Stack them carefully somewhere out of the way, as they will be useful later for covering the edges of the pond.

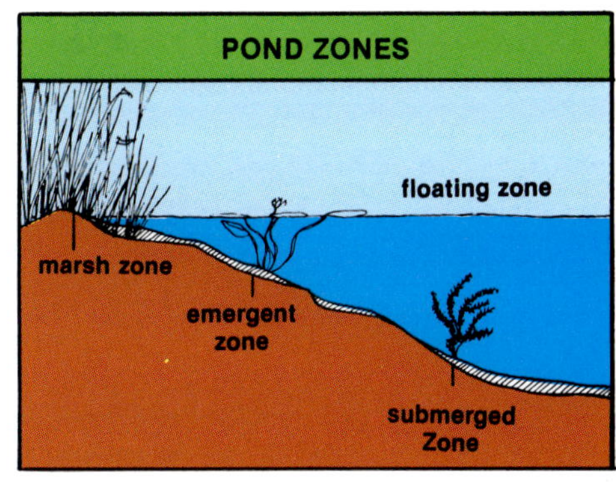

It is a good idea to have everybody involved in the project lift at least a few spadefuls of earth, as evidence of commitment; so they know how it feels, and so that they can all say that they helped to dig it. This is particularly true of children: however young, they should all be encouraged to make at least a token effort. It shouldn't be an adults-only enterprise. Make sure someone brings a camera and everyone gets photographed doing their bit. Why not contact the local paper and get the Mayor or Mayoress photographed lifting a shoveful or two?

In order not to let anyone over-exert themselves, change the digging, carrying and dumping teams regularly. Try each job yourself to find out just how hard each task is. You will probably be surprised how heavy the work is, particularly if you have a clay soil to dig out. It is always a good idea to get the digging phase over as quickly as

DRAINING A CONCRETE POND

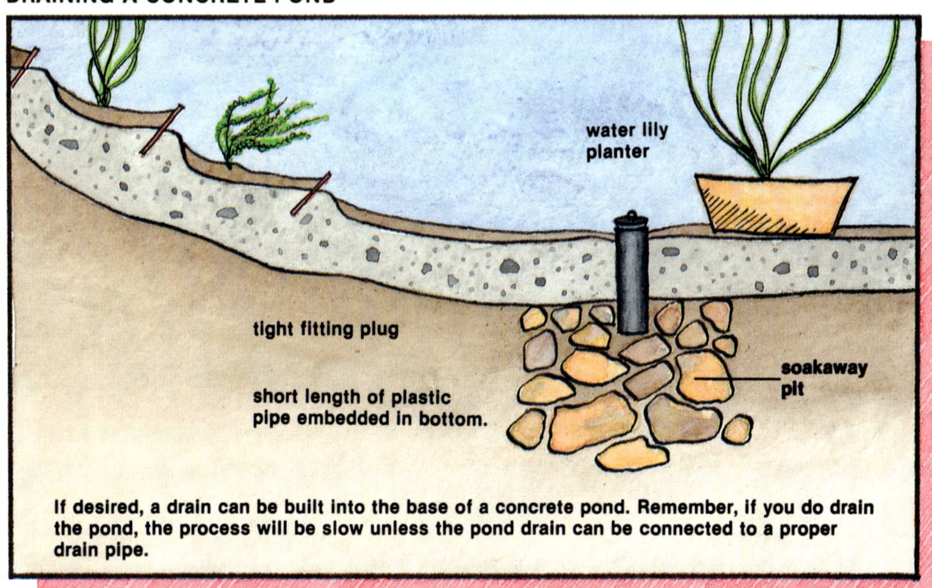

If desired, a drain can be built into the base of a concrete pond. Remember, if you do drain the pond, the process will be slow unless the pond drain can be connected to a proper drain pipe.

possible — for one thing, it is less likely to rain if you take only a couple of days. It may seem ironic to have to empty a pond in order to get on with constructing it, but it stops being funny and becomes tiresome very soon, and also quickly decreases the enthusiasm of the builders. In fact, the longer the project takes, the more enthusiasm will decline. If the pond is a big one and bound to take a long time, try to do it in clear-cut stages, and hold team competitions for best progress in an hour or similar events. Try to make the digging as much fun as possible. For a school pond, use every opportunity for impromptu teaching — surface to volume ratios, soil profiles, roots, life in the soil, the origins of any objects discovered, previous history of the site, anything and everything to break up the routine.

Always dig a little deeper than you plan the pond to be to allow for the lining and any sediment. Check the depth and slope profile regularly, as it is easier to get it right first time than to amend it later. Compact the pond base carefully, especially for glass fibre or concrete lining.

Have your lining material ready to hand before the digging is finished. Not only is it frustrating to have to wait for it but imagine how you would feel if the pond filled up overnight before the lining material arrived.

Stages in digging your pond

1. Mark out the shape and size on the grass with string, then chalk or paint.
2. Remove turves and stack for use later as edging.

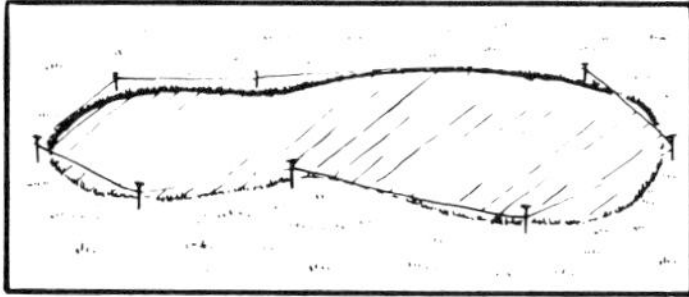

3. Check for level.
(a) Put tight strings across from pegs near the 'corners'. Tie or stick the strings so they do not slip up or down the pegs. For large ponds an extra central peg and additional strings are required. Tap in pegs until all strings are horizontal, tested using a builders' spirit level.

(b) Decide how far below string level you want the pond top (base of path or edging) to be. Mark sticks out with paint or waterproof felt pen, as shown. Knock in sticks near the corner pegs until their tops are just at string level, and add further sticks similarly marked anywhere on the outside strings, all at the same level. Keep these level markers just outside the area to be dug out. Finally remove the strings and corner pegs. Your marker sticks will tell you the level to dig to, even on a sloping site.

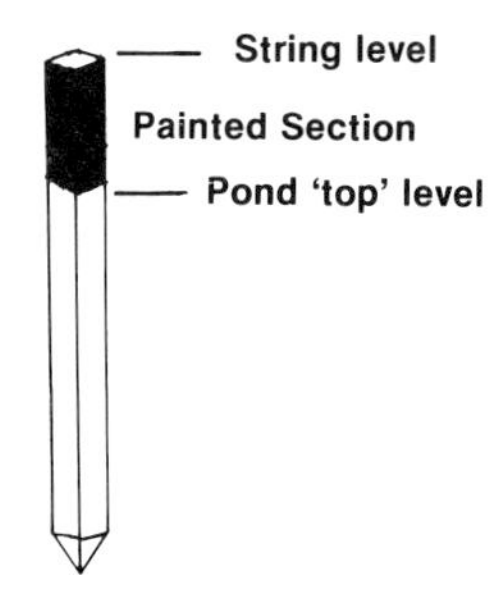

4. Decide on the main edge profile you want. Make a template from a piece of hardboard, cut full size to the pattern you want.

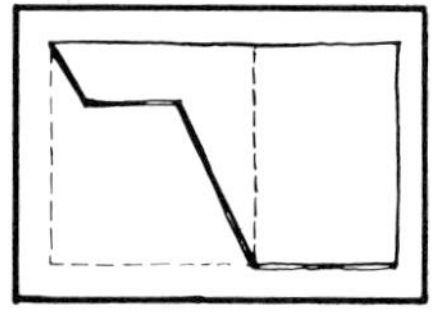

Use this as you dig to get the pond sides correctly sloped. (Examples of profiles are shown on the plans in chapter 2). Remember the margin shelf does not have to run all the way round the pond, but the sides should slope inwards at about 20° to avoid later subsidence. For safety, try to include one more gently sloping edge.

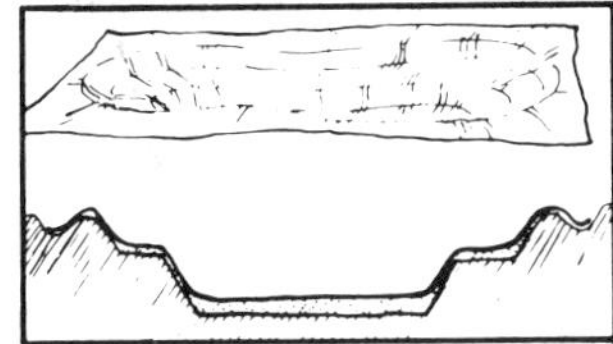

5. Dig out the hole, then smooth the sides and remove any sharp stones, etc. Cover the base and edges (after compacting with many pairs of feet) with about 3cm of sand. If using a liner, spread damp sand up the pond sides, or use layers of old newspaper, an old carpet, underfelt, plastic sheeting or even old fertiliser bags. This layer is to protect the liner from stones which may work out of the soil once water is put in the liner, and if your soil is stony, you may want to use a sand layer **and** old carpet, etc. for greater security.

Make sure the carpet layer extends over the edges of the pond and is continuous.

If you have the money, commercially produced protective sheeting is available for the same purpose.

Lining your pond

This is the part of the project that takes most skill and care.

Glassfibre or rigid plastic ponds

If you are using a rigid liner, GRP or a shaped plastic pool for example, make sure that it is the best fit possible by sculpting the hole and infilling where necessary. If it sags badly when filled, the edges will lift and it will probably crack eventually. It is worth the time and trouble to get it right first time.

Concrete lined ponds

If you are using concrete, try and obtain the services of someone skilled in casting concrete to supervise. The diagrams on pages 14 and 15 show a suitable approach to constructing your pond with concrete (ask friends, local authorities, neighbours, parents, anyone to help here).

An alternative method is to make the walls and base of the pond by laying down successive layers of heavy fabric, (e.g. old carpet) and concrete. Several layers are required but build up rapidly to form a laminated wall. Finish with a final, thicker layer of concrete to be sure it is waterproof. Soak the fabric first to make sure the concrete bonds firmly to it and try not to crack it during the early stages. This method may sound odd but has the advantage that it is easy to form curves, bulges and slopes. If you are casting concrete, you may have to substitute steps for slopes.

Remember, new concrete contains toxic substances that have to be flushed out by filling and then changing the water after a few days.

Once your concrete pond has been flushed through a couple of times it can be planted. It is a good idea to put a thin layer of soil in the bottom of the pond to provide nutrients and a substrate for bottom living organisms and rooted plants. Better still is to put in some mud and water from an existing, well established pond — it will contain seeds, eggs and the resting stages of many small organisms to get your pond off to a good start.

dragonfly larva

50mm

SECTIONAL VIEW OF A POND (CONSTRUCTED WITH A POND LINER)

Constructing the edge of a pond.

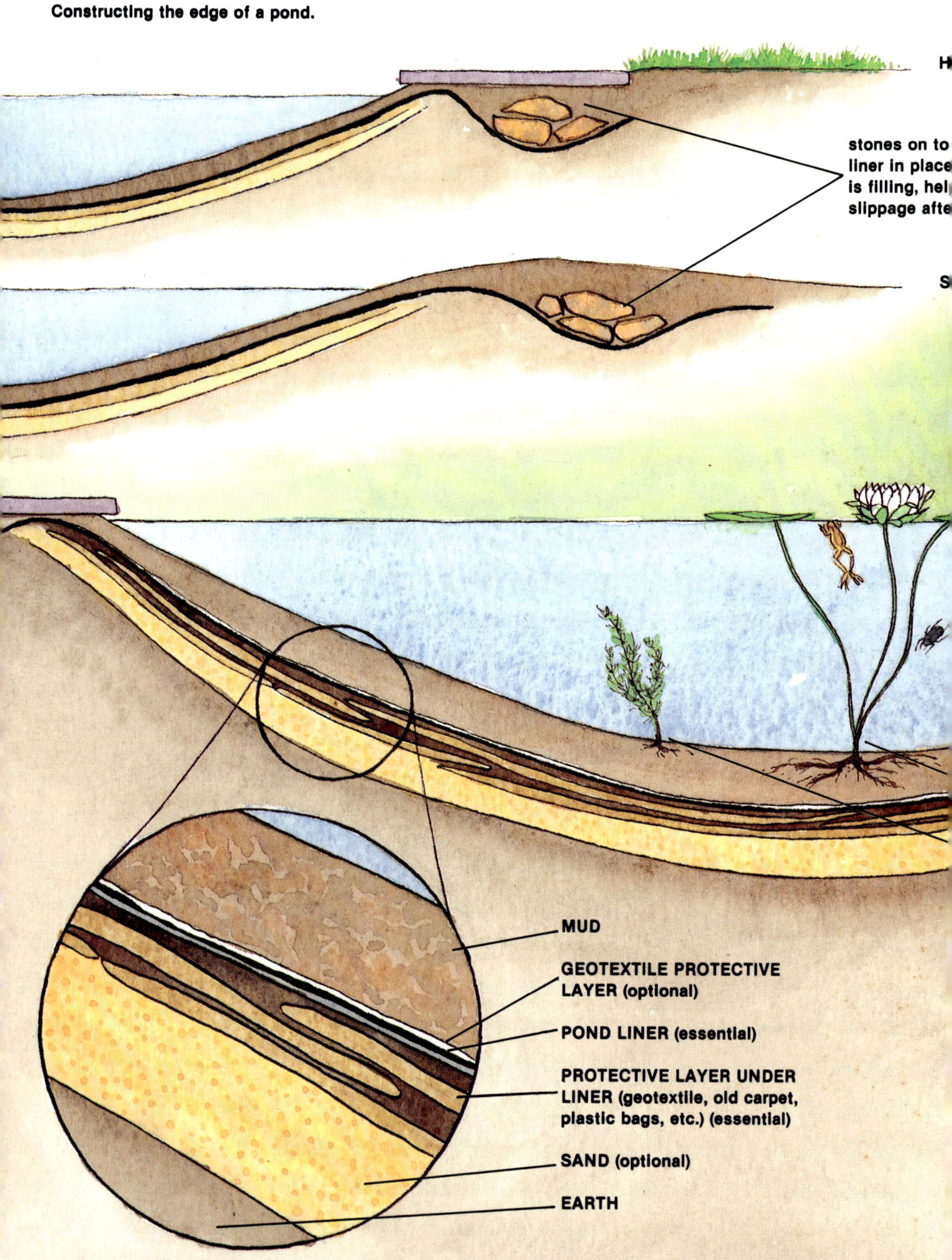

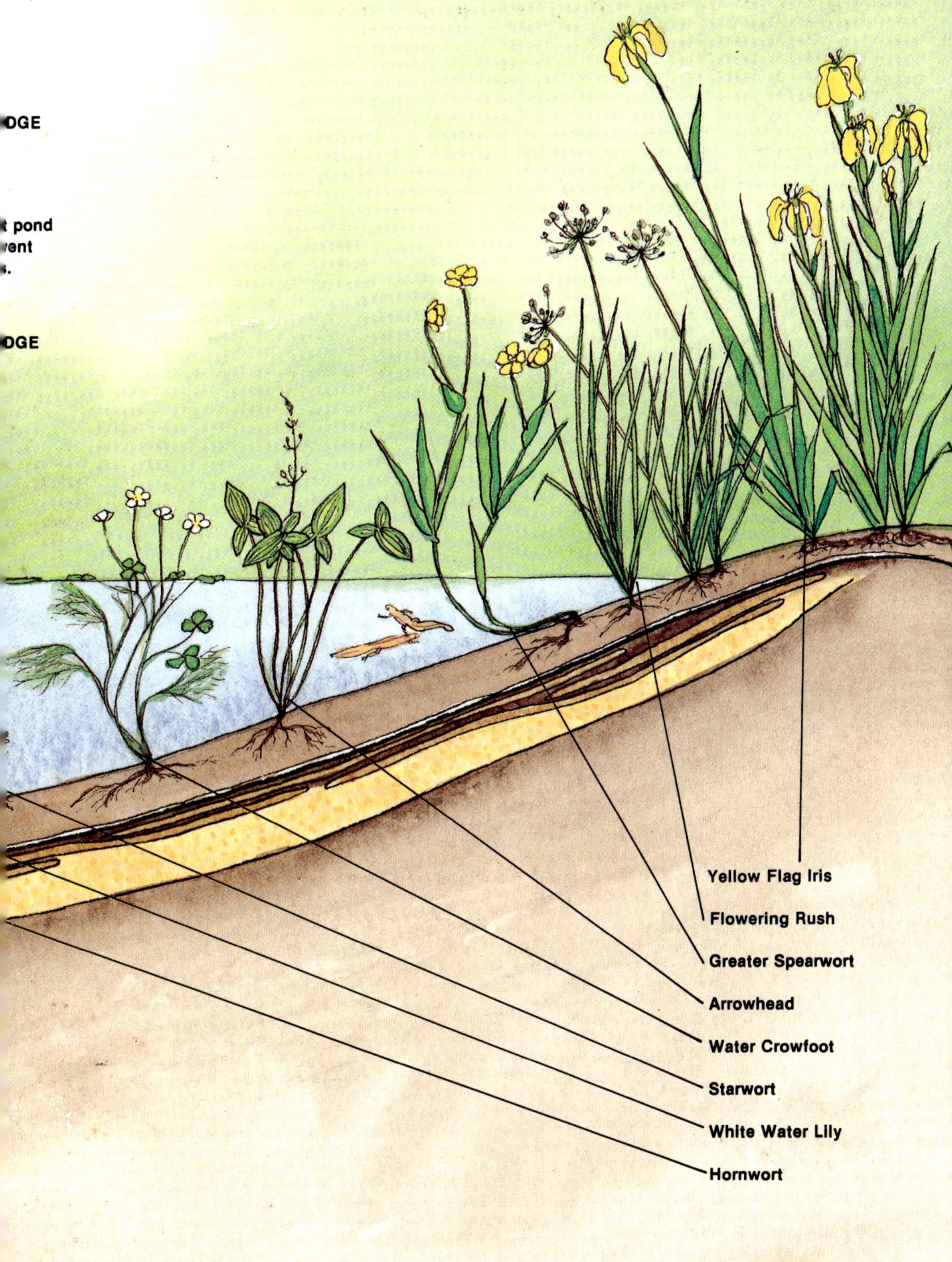
DGE
pond
ent
s.
DGE
Yellow Flag Iris
Flowering Rush
Greater Spearwort
Arrowhead
Water Crowfoot
Starwort
White Water Lily
Hornwort

Flexible plastic or butyl rubber lined ponds

If you have chosen to use a liner in your pond, then this is the exciting part, after much sweat and backache. There are two slightly different approaches; first the **fill and plant later** method . . .

1. First, lift an extra line of turves from around the edge of your pond and prepare a trench about 15 to 20cm deep on this line.

2. Unroll the liner and spread it across the pond cavity; the more hands here the better. Try and get a reasonably even overlap around the pond edges and remember, you need more overlap where the pond is deepest. Let the liner sag into the pond cavity to check that it will fit correctly. Ideally you should have at least 50cm overlap all the way round.

   Assuming it fits, lay it flat across the pond cavity and stretch it on all sides a little, weighing it down on the edges with stones or bricks. These anchor the liner and will be 'dragged' towards the hole as the liner sags into it, so place them evenly and so they will not overhang the excavation.

3. Fetch the hose and turn it on (at last). As the liner fills it will gradually sag into the hole, stretching a little and also pulling the anchor stones inward. Most wrinkles will disappear, but those remaining will be covered by soil or plants later. Continue until the pond is full and the liner is moulded to the sides of the excavation.

4. Bed the liner in around the edge. This is why you lifted turves from around the edge and prepared your trench. Put the free edges of the liner into the trench and weigh them down with the stones or bricks, then level off with soil. If you have a lot of liner left, you can fold the edges loosely back into the pond (it helps to protect the liner) or cut off the surplus pieces if you prefer. Where there are awkward folds, nick the edges so that the material lies flat to the ground. Remember to leave a run-off channel so that excess water has a way out — to a soakaway or a boggy area.

5. Replace the turves, covering the edge of the pond and sloping down into the water to give a natural effect, or lay flagstones down around part of the edge to allow dry access. The flagstones should slightly overlap the pond edge (about 5cm), and slope very slightly down *away* from the pond edge. This is an important safety feature where children will make regular use of the pond. Flagstones should preferably be carefully bedded in sand and mortar, and joints should be filled with mortar to prevent plant growth — this is one place where safety comes before a natural finish!

6. Turn your beautifully clear pond into mud soup! Put in shovelfuls of sieved soil (no stones of course) so as to cover the base and the shelves of the pond fairly evenly to a depth of 5cm. Try to get some soil onto the sloping walls, and make sure you cover the edges above the water line to hide the liner from the sun. Leave to settle, then start planting, using baskets or directly into the soil layer. Left alone, the pond will clear in a few days at most and oxygenating (submerged) plants will complete the job.

Some pond builders advise a layer of protective sheeting on top of the liner. This does help but has one drawback, apart from the cost. If this sheeting is laid over the whole liner, including the edges of the pond, it tends to act like a wick, drawing water from the pond by capillary action and passing it to the surrounding soil. If it is only laid in the bottom of the pond this cannot happen, but it tends to slip down the sloping sides. For this reason I recommend simple sieved soil.

Now for the other method — **plant before filling . . .**

Dig the surround trench as before, but this time lower the liner into the hole and *leave* it there. Carefully push the liner into the corners (folding a little if necessary) and up the walls. At the surface place stones on the liner edges to hold them firm. Now, while the pond is still dry, put in the sieved soil on the base, up the walls and on the shelves. Spray water on the soil a little to help it stick. Now place your plant baskets as required, and put the rooted plants directly in the soil layer. If using several plant baskets, you may decide to add a soil layer only to parts of the shelves and pond base. You can add a submersible pump for fountain and/or cascade at this point if your design calls for it.

Once you are satisfied, then you are ready to fill the pond. It is easiest to use a hose for this, the end placed on a weighted plastic sheet in the lowest part of the pond so as to minimise disturbance of the soil layer. If you tie a string to the plastic sheet, you won't have to dive for it later.

Now is a good time to organise a sweepstake on how long it will take the pond to fill. If you don't have a hose you can try a bucket chain: if you have to fill it this way, try counting the buckets, it will help to pass the time.

Check the liner as the pond fills. It will settle into the shape of the hole, pulling the edges in a bit. Liners will stretch a little to fill the minor hollows or spread over bulges.

When the pond is getting full and the liner has settled to nearly its full extent you can start to bed it in around the edge trench, and lay turves and paving stones as detailed above.

Which approach should you choose? The second is probably best for butyl liners, but either will work. PVC liners, being more stretchy, may settle better using the first method. Either way, the pond will be murky for a while.

To give your pond a good start, try to put in a bucket of water and some mud from an existing healthy pond. This will add minibeasts, eggs and seeds, but nature (courtesy of wind and birds) will do the same thing given time.

lesser waterboatman

|← 13mm →|

4. Settling and Stocking

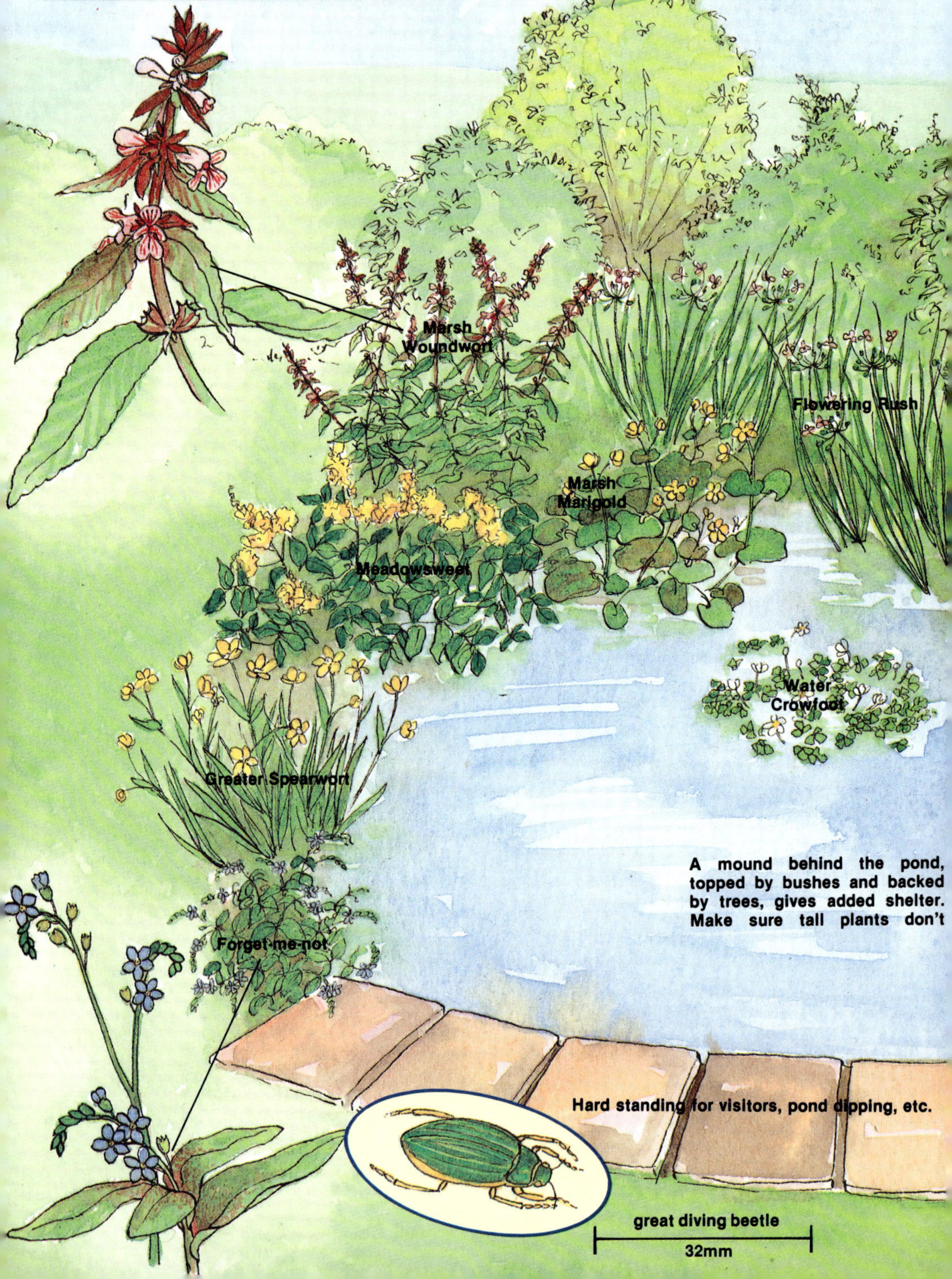

Marsh Woundwort
Flowering Rush
Marsh Marigold
Meadowsweet
Water Crowfoot
Greater Spearwort
Forget-me-not
Hard standing for visitors, pond dipping, etc.
great diving beetle
32mm

A mound behind the pond, topped by bushes and backed by trees, gives added shelter. Make sure tall plants don't

Flowering Rush
Yellow Flag Iris
Water Mint
Marsh Marigold
Purple Loosestrife
shadow the pond too much;
leave the south side open.
(Fencing not shown)
Speedwell
Butterbur
stickleback
60mm

Settling

At first, new ponds look unattractive. The water will be muddy, may have scum on top and will very soon turn green. Don't worry, this happens to all ponds. The mud will settle, the water clear and pond animals start to appear. Your pond will never be crystal clear, resembling a mountain tarn; if it is there is something wrong. A clear pond is a lifeless pond. It should not, however, smell. This happens to a pond with an excess of organic matter in it, which dies and decays, causing the smell. Your aim should be to strike a balance between plants, animals and open water for the best effect.

If you are not convinced of the need for some sediment and murkiness, some 'untidy' fringing vegetation and soft, muddy pond edges, and instead picture a hard edged pond with clear water, a couple of artistically placed exotic water lilies and brightly coloured fish circling a central fountain, consider the following analogy. A natural pond is like a meadow, full of a variety of wild flowers and alive with bees, butterflies and insects. All it needs is to be mowed annually to maintain this life. An ornamental pond is like a lawn, limited to a few species of plants, most of which are considered to be weeds and discouraged and very few animal species. In order to maintain its existence, it has to be fertilised, treated with weed killer, spiked, seeded and rolled and cut regularly.

Although any pond is better than none, a *natural* wildlife pond holds far more than an ornamental one, and is easier to maintain. If you want goldfish and a fountain, why not build two ponds, one of each kind?

Stocking a wildlife pond

Three types of large plants are found in ponds, corresponding to the pond zones shown on page 15: **emergent, floating leaved** and **submerged. Damp loving plants** also grow around the edges of the pond, (especially if a marsh zone is available) and contribute towards its visual effect, but these are not truly pond plants.

Emergent plants
These have their roots in water but lift their leaves above it. Familiar examples will be *reeds* and *watercress.*

Floating leaved plants
These are rooted plants, which have floating leaves and flowers, or they raise their flowers a little above the surface. *Water lilies* are the prime example.

Submerged plants
These grow wholly or substantially beneath the surface. A few bear flowers above the surface though they have submerged leaves and stems. Familiar examples are the many *waterweeds.*

Other plants found in ponds are the *algae,* which include microscopic, floating forms that frequently turn pond water green, or filamentous forms, the thin green threads which coat the sides of ponds and grow on plant stems. *Seaweeds* are algae too but no such large algae grow in fresh water.

Also found in ponds are the non-rooted floating plants: *duckweeds, frogbit, water soldier* and *water hyacinth.* These can get to be a problem as they grow so fast.

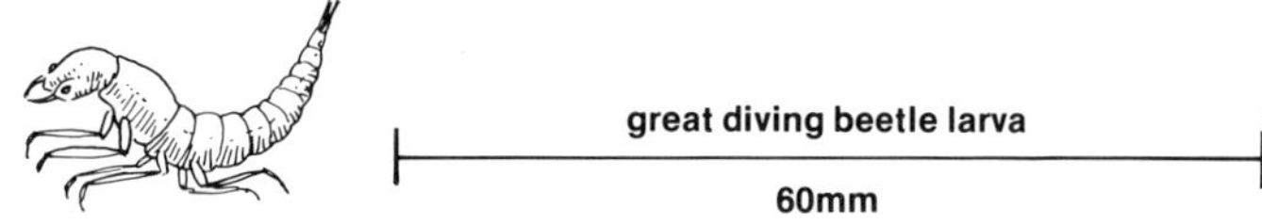

The following list will help you in stocking your pond.

<table>
<tr><td valign="top">

FRINGING/MARSH PLANTS

Recommended

Forget-me-not (Myosotis sps.)

Marsh Marigold or King Cup (Caltha palustris)

Meadowsweet (Filipendula ulmaria)

Skullcap (Scutellaria galericulata)

Purple Loosestrife (Lythrum salicaria)

Hemp Agrimony (Eupatorium cannabinum)

Greater Spearwort (Ranunculus lingua)

Marsh Woundwort (Stachys palustris)

Spear Mint (Mentha spicata)

Watermint (Mentha aquatica)

Peppermint (Mentha x piperata)

Brooklime (Veronica beccabunga)

Water Speedwell (Veronica anagallis-aquatica)

Not Recommended

Hemlock Water Dropwort (Oenanthe crocata)
extremely poisonous

EMERGENT PLANTS

Recommended

Flowering Rush (Butomus umbellatus)

Yellow Iris (Iris pseudacorus)

Arrowhead (Sagittaria sagittifolia)

Water Plantain (Alisma plantago-aquatica)

Watercress (Nasturtium officinale)

Water Violet (Hottonia palustris)

Bog Arum (Calla palustris)

** Can spread rapidly*

+ Invasive, chokes ponds

</td><td valign="top">

FLOATING LEAVED PLANTS

Recommended

Fringed Water Lily (Nymphoides peltata)

White Water Lily (Nymphaea alba)

*Amphibious Bistort * (Polygonum amphibium)*

Frogbit (Hydrocharis morsus-ranae)

Water Crowfoot (Ranunculus aquatilis)

Not Recommended

Foreign waterlilies

Duckweed + (Lemna sps.)

Water-fern + (Azolla filiculoides)

Water Hyacinth +
a tropical waterweed that chokes lakes and rivers; frost kills it

SUBMERGED PLANTS

Recommended

Hornwort (Ceratophyllum demersum)

Water Milfoil (Myriophyllum spicatum)

Bladderwort, a carnivorous plant (Utricularia vulgaris)

Water Starwort (Callitriche stagnalis)

Not Recommended

Canadian Pondweed, (Elodea, Anacharis) +

New Zealand Pondweed (Pygmyweed) +

EMERGENT PLANTS

Not Recommended

Greater Reedmace +
often wrongly called Bullrush
(Typha latifolia)
Unbranched Burreed + (Sparganium simplex)
Marestail + (Hippuris vulgaris)
Common Reed + (Phragmites australis)

</td></tr>
</table>

Planting — Notes

Try to bed all fringing marsh plants in well so that they do not become dislodged by the wind. Once they become established this will seldom be a problem: clumps of plants tend to support each other as their roots link to form a network. When planting consider the eventual **height** that the plants grow to. For example, the *common reed (Phragmites australis)* can reach a height of nearly twelve feet (3.5 metres), though is unlikely to do so in a small pond. (This plant is the 'Norfolk reed' which makes the best quality thatching material).

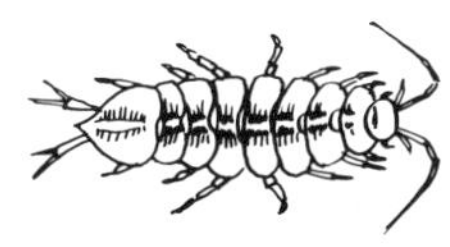

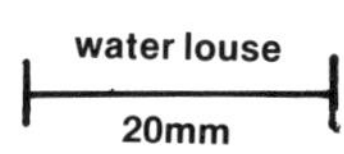

Emergent Plants

Arrowhead

Water Violet

Yellow Flag Iris

Water Plantain

Bog Arum

... more plants on pages 34/35

It may be better to plant lower growing reeds, rushes and sedges around the edge of your pond (in a marsh area or on the shelf). Attractive species are *flowering rush* which grows to about 1.5 metres and *yellow flag iris,* about 1.2 metres. If you feel no pond is complete without *reedmace* (often called bullrush) with its distinctive club-shaped flower heads, then try to plant the *lesser reedmace (Typha augustifolia)* rather than the *great reedmace (Typha latifolia)* as it is better scaled to a small pond and less rampant. Thin out regularly, or your pond will fill up with reeds!

Also on the pond shelf, try *arrowhead, water crowfoot, water violet* and *amphibious bistort.* Good marsh plants which like to 'get their feet wet' are *marsh marigold* and *greater spearwort,* which are both members of the buttercup family; *purple loosestrife* and *marsh woundwort,* both with pinkish-purple flowers; *water mint, spear mint* and their hybrid *peppermint,* all with lilac-coloured flowers attractive to insects.

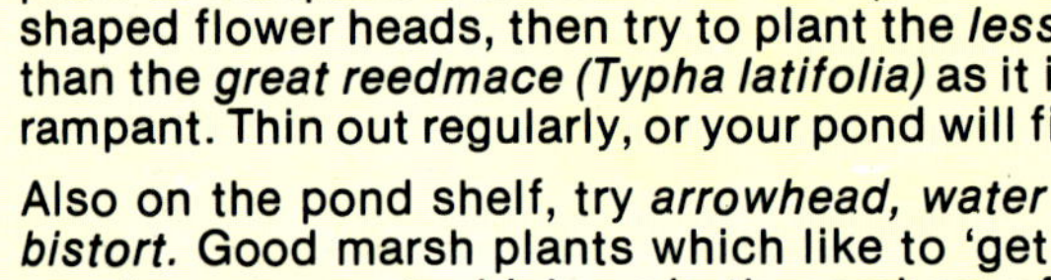

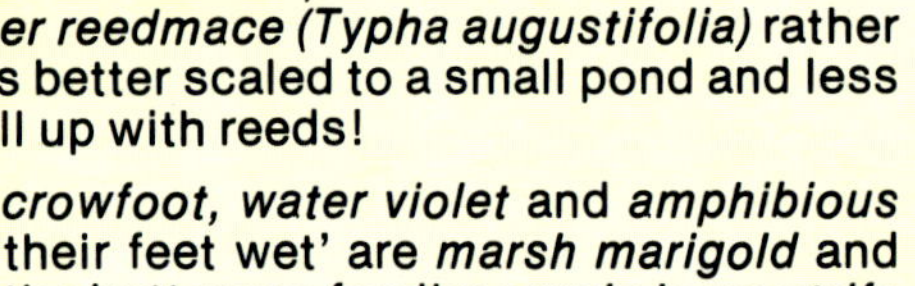

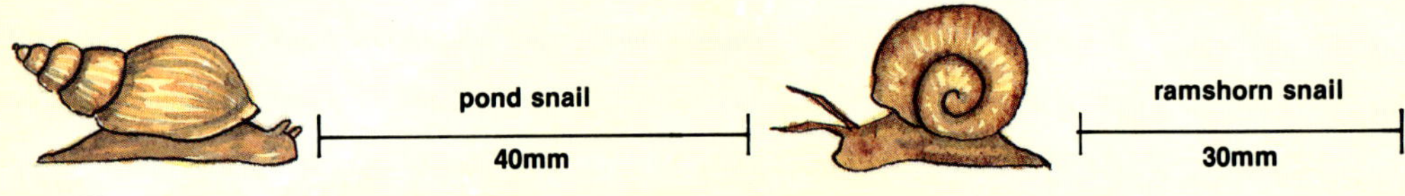

Watercress can also be grown but tends to get quickly out of hand. You can at least eat what you weed out, however!

Other attractive plants which will grow on the shelf at the edge of the pond are *forget-me-not* (there are various species including a water forget-me-not) and several species of speedwell notably *brooklime* and *water speedwell.*

A sweet smelling plant of damp meadows is *meadowsweet,* which is recommended. Not quite so highly thought of is *ramsons* or *wild garlic (Allium ursinium),* an attractive glossy green leaved plant with a head of white star shaped flowers but which smells strongly of garlic, especially if crushed.

If space allows and you would like a large interesting plant in your marsh area, try planting a specimen of *butterbur (Petasites hybridus).* The growth form is a bit like rhubarb but the leaves can grow to nearly 1 metre wide. As this species has male and female flowers on separate plants, one specimen is unlikely to seed, but as a perennial, once established it will grow every year.

Whatever you plant, there will also be natural colonisation. This usually produces a pleasant effect, but *docks, thistles* and *nettles* may have to be removed by hand if they threaten to become dominant.

The above mentioned plants are given only as a guide to planting — many others are suitable, but in general, it is advisable to avoid exotic species. Native plants tend to be better behaved towards each other. For this reason, native pond weeds (listed in the table as **submerged plants**) are preferable to (and more attractive than) Canadian pondweed or the invasive New Zealander, pygmyweed.

How to plant your pond

The best planting times are May to September — if possible May/June. Emergent plants can be planted directly into the soil layer on the pond shelf, or in shallow containers. Similarly, floating leaved and submerged plants can be put directly in the bottom soil or in larger containers.

These aquatic plant containers are now widely available in a variety of shapes and sizes. They resemble plastic washing baskets, with many holes in the sides and base. First, line the container with a square of hessian, then fill nearly to the top with soil — heavy soil is best or use ordinary garden soil. Don't use peat or sand or leafmould. Plant one or more of your aquatics firmly into the soil, allowing for growth and keeping emergent, floating leaved and submerged types in separate containers. For **water lilies,** keep the crown above soil level.

Submerged plants are usually sold as pieces — make a hole in the soil and push the lower part of the stem in, then press the soil around it firmly enough to hold it. A large container will hold (say) 15 submerged aquatics. Now add a good layer of small gravel to the surface. This helps trap the soil in the container. Slowly lower the container in the pond, so as not to dry-out the aquatic plants, but ensuring the gravel

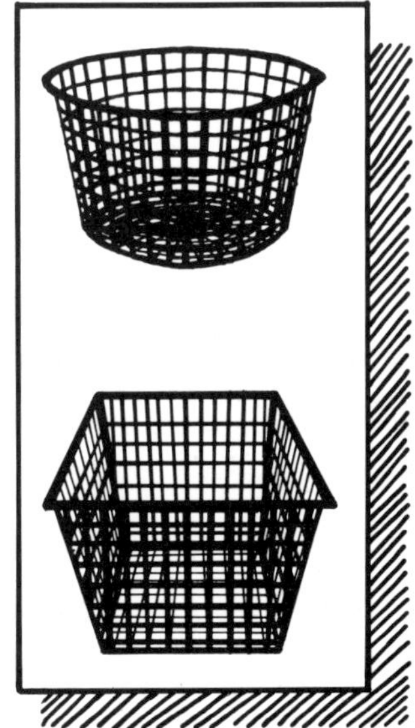

Plant containers

does not spill out. Most containers can go where you want them — remember not to cover the whole shelf and base areas since room for growth is needed — but *lilies* are best placed in a fairly shallow area (at least 45cm deep) or on bricks and gradually lowered as they grow so that their leaves always reach the surface.

For those who do not like wading, containers can be accurately placed using two stout ropes (e.g. skipping ropes). Thread a rope through each side of the container at one end of the pond so that two helpers can hold it up from opposite sides of the pond. Slowly transport it above the water to the desired spot, then sink it slowly by

relaxing the ropes together (teamwork is essential!). When settled, drop one end of each rope and pull on the other end to release it.

Containers on the shelf are easily retrieved for plant care, and those in the depths can be hauled out (with care) by use of garden rakes, so that there are certainly advantages over using direct-planting. Normally, the container itself is soon hidden by plant growth, but of course it does limit the spread of plants along the shelf or pond base.

How many plants?

As a rough guide, a new pond with a surface area of **3 square metres** might include: 2 lilies, 15 submerged (oxygenating) plants, 6 emergents.

A pond of **10 square metres** might include: 3 floating leaved/lilies, 45 submerged (oxygenating) plants, 15 emergents.

The submerged plants are most important as they provide ideal homes — and food — for many minibeasts, while keeping the water in good condition. Eventually, around *half* of the pond surface area should be covered by the various plants.

Planting the surrounds of your pond

It is a good idea to plant the area around a pond. If you do not, something will grow anyway and it will probably be docks and nettles. By choosing your fringing vegetation carefully you can restrict access to the pond to one or two areas of bank and provide cover for pond life in others. Try to plant several species to get a varied effect but do not mix them together as some species will overwhelm others. It is best to start plants off in groups or clumps of a single species until they become established and then let them grow together for a more natural effect. Planting trees and bushes around a pond helps to shelter it from wind, give a natural backdrop and help create a tranquil atmosphere but if they are too close they will create problems by dropping leaves in the pond and shading the pond from sunlight.

The **tree** species most generally associated with ponds are the various species of willow, alder and aspen. *Willows* will grow extremely vigorously and respond to pruning by producing several stems when one is cut. In this way they can be used to hide a wall quickly or provide shelter. A willow can grow 2 to 3 metres in a year. Willow regenerates so well that a cut branch driven into the ground will often take root. *Alders* grow rapidly too and will quickly form a screen or windbreak. Although a rather gloomy dark green they are usually well shaped trees and bear interesting little cone-like seed cases and catkins. *Aspens* are more delicate trees, with light green leaves that move in the slightest breeze. They provide a good contrast to alders. These three trees all like damp ground, but other trees will grow close to ponds equally well.

Of course, almost all broadleaved trees lose their leaves in winter, lessening their sheltering effect. Exceptions are *holly* and *holm oak* (evergreen oak) but both of these grow slowly. You could try *box* or *bay* however, which are both evergreen. *Conifers* can be planted; foreign hybrids often grow quickly but have little to offer wildlife except shelter. There are only three native British conifers: Scots Pine, Juniper and Yew. *Scots Pine* grows well in sandy or poor soil but has an open rather than dense branch structure. *Juniper* will grow in the harshest conditions and produces edible berries. Its dense growth provides excellent cover too, but it is slow growing. *Yew* is an excellent shelter tree but it is **not** recommended because all parts of the tree are very poisonous, especially the attractive berries.

Many sorts of **bushes** can be grown but it is best to avoid *laurels* and *rhododendrons* because they suppress the growth of other plants. *Privet* makes a surprisingly good shelter bush when it is allowed to grow; the flowers and fruit attract butterflies and birds as well. It has the advantage of being semi-evergreen though the berries are slightly poisonous to people. A very good shrub is *butcher's broom (Ruscus aculeatus)* — tough spiny, evergreen, with orange-red berries, an attractive vandal repellent.

If your pond has a wall behind or beside it, why not train a **creeper** up it? A shady wall is good for *ivy,* which is evergreen and good for wildlife. A sunlit wall is suitable for a range of climbers both native and introduced. Fences can also provide a base for climbing plants. If you have a large ugly wall or fence to cover and require rapid screening, try *Russian vine.* The only problem with this plant is that it grows almost visibly fast and never seems to stop. It will therefore require cutting back regularly.

The choice of **ground cover** around the pond depends on the degree of *tidiness* required. Poor soil is an advantage if you want to encourage meadowland wild flowers. A good way to start a new meadow is to use one of the grass/wildflower seed mixtures, which are designed to suit particular soil types. Always try to use seed of British origin.

Animals

If you introduce water, mud and plants from other ponds, small animals will come in with them. They will rapidly multiply within the pond until a balance is reached. *Insects* will usually arrive by themselves, as many of them fly. *Snails* normally arrive with pond plants but can be introduced deliberately; they are useful in keeping *filamentous algae* in check. If you have a severe problem with floating, microscopic algae turning the water green (not just a slight green tint but a pea-soup green that persists), try introducing a few *pond mussels* which feed on algae by filtering them from the water.

daphnia (waterflea)

3mm

water mite

4mm

It is best to allow your pond to settle and stock itself with animal life during its first year. You will see changes in its water, plant and animal populations and it will come to a fairly stable ecological balance. Winter is a resting period for pond life but next spring will reveal a rich population, almost certainly with unexpected species present.

If you would like to introduce any particular animals, consider the effect on the pond as a whole. Actively predatory species can clear a pond of most of its smaller animals quite quickly. This is particularly true of *fish*. *Sticklebacks* can usually be accommodated without too many problems, but *goldfish, golden orfe, koi carp* and other large fish will clear it of most other animal life. If you want to encourage *frogs, toads* and *newts* to breed in your pond then do not introduce large fish — a community of tadpoles and fish together rapidly becomes one of fat fish alone. **If you want fish, build a separate pond.**

In general, it is not a good idea to introduce **foreign** animal species to your pond. Many are unsuited to the British climate and will die, others can become a threat to native British species.

Many **land animals** may come to your pond to drink or look for food. Common visitors are *cats, dogs, foxes, rabbits* and *mice.* They may leave footprints in the mud at the pond's edge. Many birds are likely to visit, including *ducks, moorhens, wagtails, gulls, reed buntings* and, of course, *starlings, pigeons* and *sparrows. Swallows* and *house martins* may visit to collect mud for nest building and to hunt insects. *Bats* may also visit.

You may be lucky enough to get a visit from a *kingfisher,* but it is unlikely to stay.

The only mammals likely to become residents are the harmless vegetarian *water vole* or the less pleasant, omnivorous *brown rat.* However, rats are unlikely to stay unless a good source of food is nearby.

As for reptiles, *adders* prefer dry conditions and are unlikely to visit your pond. The harmless *grass snake* is much fonder of water — it belongs to the water snake family and eats a lot of frogs. Any 'snake' seen is probably not a grass snake hunting for frogs, as they are actually no longer common, but a *slowworm,* (actually a legless lizard) after slugs and snails.

The *European terrapin* can live in the British climate but only rarely is a British summer warm enough to allow it to breed. For this reason it is not native to Britain. It is carnivorous and will eat fish, frogs and other amphibians. Other terrapins are from warmer climates and will die in a British winter; they are all carnivorous.

Native British amphibians will quite likely colonise your pond naturally. If not, a jamjar of frog spawn or toad spawn, (recognisable because it is found in long strings unlike frog spawn), will fill your pond with tadpoles. *Newts* lay their eggs singly on the leaves of water-weeds so are less easy to introduce in this way. It is **illegal** to take either the *great crested newt* or the *natterjack toad* from the wild as both are endangered British species.

As previously stated, the only fish recommended for a pond are *sticklebacks. Minnows* require running water, as does the *miller's thumb;* all other British species grow too large for a small pond and will eat everything else in it.

mosquito larva

|———————|
10mm

A pond does not require much maintenance but it does need to be regularly checked for leaks, contamination and litter. If litter is removed promptly, the pond will look better and people will tend to respect it more. Litter breeds litter. A pond can become completely choked if not cleared regularly. Just as serious, overflows or pump inlets can become blocked. A blocked pump will probably burn out, necessitating repair or replacement.

It is a good idea to keep water level in a pond relatively constant for the best growth of plants and animals. Topping up can be done with tap water, though it is not ideal due to the presence of chlorine, or by any other convenient source of clean water. If chlorine builds up in the pond and affects the pond life, for example after a dry spell, oxygenating the water with an air pump, a water cascade or fountain or by regular vigorous agitation may help.

If some other form of contamination is suspected, the only real remedy is to drain the pond and refill it, after checking the bottom for any residue of contamination. In really severe cases, the sediment would have to be removed and replaced, though I have never heard of an example this bad.

In the case of a **leak,** let the water subside until the hole becomes visible. Small holes may have to be searched for. Normally, such holes can be sealed in situ, with a patch of liner material and a suitable adhesive (available from the liner supplier).

If you are unlucky and the hole is in the bottom you may have to bail out the last of the water to find it. In any case, try to refill the pond promptly; many pond creatures and plants can stand a short period of drying. If the pond dries completely for a longish period, you may get an algal bloom when it is refilled. This is because drying a pond tends to release nutrients from the bottom sediments; it also kills many of the larger plants which would compete with the algae for the nutrients in a normal situation. Like other algal blooms, this is a self-correcting condition, though removing filamentous algae (blanket weed) can help. The removed algae can be composted, as can any pond vegetation.

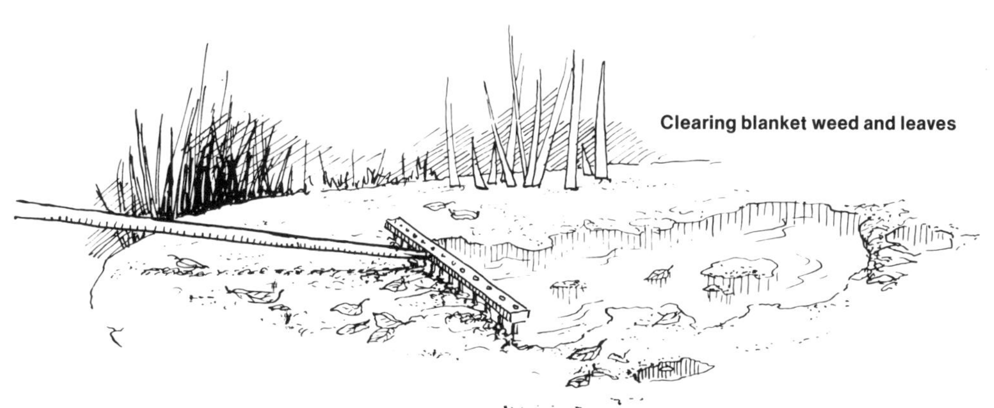

Clearing blanket weed and leaves

The most important regular maintenance job occurs only in autumn; this is the clearance of fallen leaves from the pond. If there has been a good growth of fringing or submerged vegetation during the summer, a large part of this should be cleared. It will grow back rapidly next spring. The above-water parts of reeds and rushes can be substantially cut back too. They will die in the winter anyway and regrow from the root stocks. Such clearance may not be necessary at the end of the pond's first year or even its second but will almost certainly be a regular job thereafter. If neglected, the pond water may become stagnant, the animals die, or the pond's open water disappear completely.

Just as a meadow needs mowing or a garden needs weeding, so a pond requires an annual clearance to maintain its condition. Under natural conditions it is the fate of all lowland ponds to fill with vegetation, become marshes, then carse (alder) woods and eventually, mixed broadleaf woodland. This is the process known as *succession.* However, one regular clearance a year is sufficient to maintain a healthy, balanced pond, full of aquatic life.

A pond is an almost completely self-contained ecosystem with a complex web of relationships between the organisms inhabiting it. A pond changes daily, seasonally and annually. Changes also occur year by year showing ecological succession in action.

Ponds show clearly the effect of weather conditions and of man's influence on natural ecosystems. All of these facets of a pond can be directly related to individual levels of the Attainment Targets for Science in the National Curriculum.

AT 1 Level 3 — pond building sequence
Building and planning work will provide input to several parts of level 3. Diaries of the process of pond construction can be kept by all the children and used as the basis of a 'How to Build a Pond' book.

AT 1 Levels 1, 2 and 3 — pond observation
For infants, a visit to a pond, when they are encouraged to look, listen, feel and smell, adds to their direct experience of the world. Discussing and describing, then and afterwards, develops their powers of description and communication. For older children this can naturally lead to measurement, comparisons, the recording of observations and the use of simple instruments to aid these procedures.

AT 1 Levels 1 to 3; AT 2 Levels 1 to 5 — pond dipping
Even if a pond cannot be visited on a regular basis but only occasionally, it is still extremely useful. One or two pond dipping sessions can provide the necessary material for fulfilling a large part of both AT 1 Levels 1 — 3, and AT 2 levels 1 — 5. The addition of diagnostic keys and of simple experiments can increase the amount of coverage of AT 2.

AT 2 Levels 1 to 5 — variety of life
The possibilities of using ponds to meet the needs of AT 2 should be fairly self-evident, but in particular living things responding to seasonal and daily changes (level 3) and items 1 and 4 of level 5 are particularly suitable. If an algal bloom appears, this could be used to meet item 3 of level 5.

AT 4 Levels 4 and 6 — pond species, variations
An established pond should provide enough individuals of various species to demonstrate variations in living organisms, and it may be possible to indicate the source of this variation — particularly in plants.

AT 5 Level 2 and 3 — pond building
Keeping a diary satisfies one of the requirements of level 2 and pond construction is certainly a project to help improve the local environment that has produced a change in the earth's surface by 'human activity', which fulfills level 3.

AT 5 Levels 2, 3 and 5 — changes in the pond, decay
Keeping a diary of changes in the pond over the year is a very valuable exercise, (photographs may provide a stimulus). Maintenance work, over-use or vandalism may produce noticeable changes and any local pollution can be discussed and its effects noted.

AT 6 Level 4 — materials
During pond construction, a useful comparison of materials can be made which is helpful in meeting the requirements of level 4.

AT 9 Levels 2, 3 and 4 — weather
The effects of weather on a pond, daily and seasonally, could be a part of a pond diary and would help in fulfilling all of AT 9. In particular, evaporation and resulting change of level in the pond ought to aid an understanding of the water cycle.

AT 13 Level 6 — the sun
The vital role of the sun can be demonstrated by reference to a pond 'awaking' in spring after the quiescence of winter.

AT 15 Level 1 — colour
The role of colour in flowers and in pond animals (camouflage, warning and mimicry) is easily demonstrated.

AT 16 Level 1 — seasons
Seasonal changes due to the weather are easily observed in the small world of a pond, on a scale readily comprehensible to children. The seasonal rhythms of life are particularly strongly marked in the life cycle of the frog and in other smaller pond animals as well as in pond plants.

Other N.C. Subject Areas

Many other links will come to mind: use string to show square metres and so find the pond's surface area; map the pond using this grid; sample soil colours/contents at different levels during construction; log air/water temperatures . . . . your pond will be an invaluable resource.

Safety Notes — for school ponds

1. Put a fence and gate round the pond to control access.
2. Allow children into the pond area only with adult supervision.
3. Insist on no running near the pond, and no fingers in water unless permitted! (Frogs are powerful magnets to little fingers).
4. Make the pond edges long enough to accommodate a class/group without crowding. Consider using non-slip concrete paving slabs, and slope these slightly away from the pond. The slabs should just overhang the pond edge.
5. Allow no more children in the area than can easily be accommodated.
6. Consider a gradual slope on accessible sides of your pond. This makes wading out easier. The deep area need not cover all the pond base, of course.
7. After dipping, specimens should be returned to the pond and containers/hands washed well in clean water.
8. Ponds with a deep section do not need winter ice layers broken, so dangerous temptations to slide on the ice can be avoided by keeping the pond area locked up.
9. Check with the LEA for further safety advice/rules.

Pond Plants

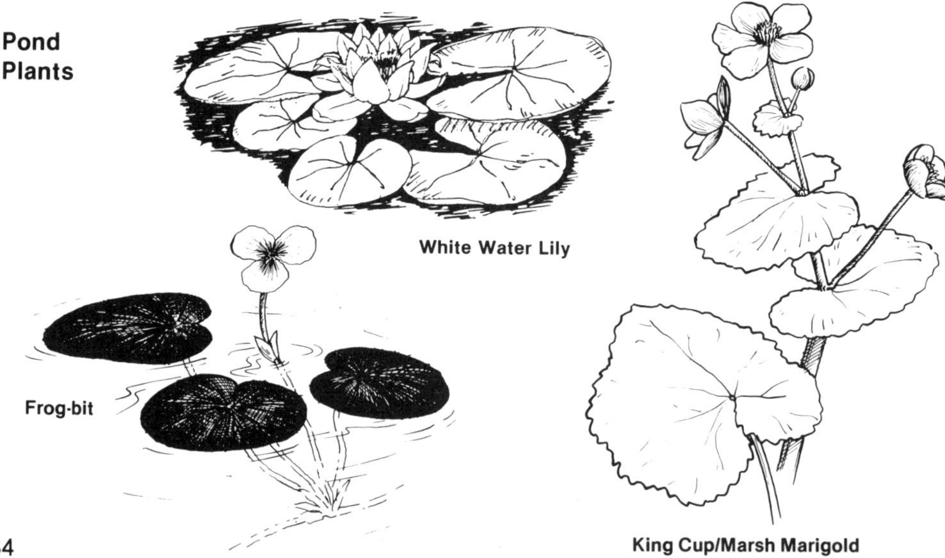